How Many

Jack Beers

There are three blue bears and three green bears.

How many bears in all?

There are four thin rings and three thick rings.

How many rings in all?

There are four sitting dogs and five standing dogs.

How many dogs in all?

How many jacks in all?